Post Scripts:

Behind the Counter
at the Ithaca Post Office

Rob Sullivan

Wasteland Press

www.wastelandpress.net
Shelbyville, KY USA

Post Scripts:
Behind the Counter at the Ithaca Post Office
by Rob Sullivan

First Printing – April 2019
ISBN: 978-1-68111-301-2
Original crow artwork on front cover
and chapter pages by Lily Armstrong-Davies.
Cover design and colorization by Nina Widger.
Author photo by Laura Taylor.

Printed in the U.S.A.

0   1   2   3   4   5   6   7   8

*To my wife Nancy, with love and gratitude
for her support at the end of my career and into retirement.*

ACKNOWLEDGMENTS

I have so many people to thank for this book. Writing it was the easy part. How do I appreciate you all?

Peter Brooks took on the arduous task of typing and formatting the original draft.

Katherine A. May, friend and fellow poet, encouraged my writing process over many breakfasts at the State Diner.

Irene Zahava inspired me to write this book after hearing some of my initial poems, then assisted with editing the first draft.

Carolyn Clark was my final editor and guide into the world of publishing.

Lily Armstrong-Davies created the original crow artwork for the book. Vikki Armstrong provided ideas for the cover design. Nina Widger colorized the cover art. Laura Taylor captured the image of the author.

Nancy Spero, my wife, assisted regularly with typing, editing, and proofreading as the drafts unfolded. Nancy was my main inspiration. She pushed, pulled, and lifted me up during the whole process of writing this book.

Lastly, I thank my co-workers, family, and friends who are part of my story. Their names and small details were sometimes changed to protect their anonymity. Special thanks goes out to Mike, Matt, Steve, Joan, Barbara, Sandy, Gary, Tony, Owen, Twinkle, Greg, Pat, Brenda, and Liz. Their patience and support were indispensable.

CONTENTS

SHAPE UP OR SHIP OUT

BEAUTY TAKES ONE'S BREATH

A LIFE OF SERVICE

MUTED MUSINGS

INTRODUCTION

Possibly the Postal Service was in my DNA. Many of my relatives followed the same path. I carried newspapers as a boy. It was my job at Boy Scout camp to deliver the mail. Sorting mail at my dorm was one of my many work-study positions that helped me pay my way through college.

Music and dance were also part of my make-up. They were the common denominators through which I could connect to others. I had been dancing socially for fourteen years when I secured a position at the Post Office in Ithaca, NY. Some customers referred to me as the "Dancing Postman."

For seven years before and eleven years after my start date, I was a disc jockey on WVBR in Ithaca. The opportunity to share my love for many types of music on the radio spilled over into the soundtrack at our post office. Upon my retirement I have returned to radio.

For most of my career I relished being able to serve the public. It was an honor and a joy. The customers were very special to me. I miss them and all my co-workers, who taught me more than they will ever know. Their desire to serve was a constant source of inspiration.

This book takes you through my career in the Postal Service. The years were 1985 to 2013. I have endeavored to include some of the highs and lows of those twenty-seven years. Enjoy the journey.

Journey
Begins

Grateful Dead Medicine

The Post Office exam
coincided with
a magical Dead concert
bringing life and hope
to thousands of merry pranksters
gathered in Barton Hall.

So it seemed that day
only fitting, in Ithaca
home of the Big Red,
to wear three T-shirts,
each embodying a unique icon:
crow,
skull,
dancing bear.

Anointing came among hundreds
of applicants for civil service,
the hard-won score was just enough
to secure a position four years on.

That night
the spring of eighty-one
was time to dance and celebrate
the poetry, the melodies,
the communal bond and cherished dream.

Pregame Prayer on North Tioga Street

Heavenly Father, Mother Earth
Buddhas, bodhisattvas, saints, and sages
I come with Ma Bell at my back
to offer up this challenge.

My task, if I choose to accept it,
is to provide for my family.
I'm willing to give part of my soul
that they might have a better life.

I've seen the way clerks greet the public.
I can and I will do better, if given the chance.
They'll get more than their money's worth
from me — every day.

Allow me to break into the lineup,
grant me a shot in training camp.
I will learn the system,
I'll exceed all expectations —
put me in, coach!

The Most Motivated Applicant

This was *the* job,
the one I wanted most.
My persistence bordered on pest-hood.
Never had any applicant
gone to such lengths.

Here I was a guest uninvited
who haunted by day, checking back in
every other month for four years
before the mast was raised
on my apprentice ship.

The Longest Interview

At long last interior views
were being revealed
shared, expounded, exposed, exercised
as options for disclosure and disclaimer.

Mission statements
dovetailed with corporal
and spiritual ethics of work-a-day
practices, procedures, decorum.

Can-do attitude versus
vice, can't do practices,
ground rules delineated
visionary service aspirations,

shining meteoric
metaphors simply assimilating,
similes bring like-minded thinking
to a harmonic convergence:

Interviewee and interviewer
found someone who would listen,
who would hear, intuit
each other's wishes, compromises, intentions.

So You Want to Be a Window Clerk

In the middle of the longest interview
there was a tapping, tapping
on the office door:
like a giant raven
he perched over me.

The Window Supervisor was
angular, hovering,
ready to swoop down
on unsuspecting volunteers.

For, contrary to most offices,
being a window clerk
in busy, cosmopolitan Ithaca
was actually a thing to be
feared and reviled.

First Slip Up

A present was left on the sidewalk.
Guru dog had given another lesson
on how composite things decompose:
manure doth occur.

Falling, on my first day,
brown-stained work pants
brought home for a costume change
and thus the first of many late rings,
punching the time clock.

Autumn rain brought
a slick, sleek, slippery
reminder: perfection's
a work in progress.

Do You Like Christmas?

Long hours extend to longer days,
weeks quadruple into months.
Ton upon ton of mail moved
in trays, each sixty to one hundred pounds,
weighing up to eight hundred pounds per cage,
all wheeled to sorting cases
for individual carrier routes.

Four, six, eight, ten, twelve hours a day
starting times of one-thirty a.m., three, four, five,
six, seven, nine or noon.
My crucial first ninety days — provisional status —
working despite colds and flu,
saying "yes" to all.
Insubordination — ill advised.

In the midst of my first holiday gauntlet
a carrier asked, "Do you like Christmas?"
My reply, "Yes."
"Good, enjoy this one,
it's the last one you'll ever like."

Don't Tell Me What Kind of Morning to Have

Clerks began early,
hours before dawn,
fed, caffeinated, sugared up
long before carriers entered.
This running start meant
biorhythms were not always in sync.

During my first week of work
my perkiness quotient
far outstripped one ornery carrier
who turned a corner
and brought me up short.

In all my manic energy
I said, "Good Morning!"
to which he replied,
"*Don't ever*, tell me
what kind of morning to have!"

The next morning
at the same time
we met again,
I simply said "Morning."
To which he replied
"*Don't ever*, tell —"
I cut him off short,
"I didn't tell you what kind
of morning to have:
I learn."

And we never did have another disagreement.

Ninety Days Before the Mast

Maiden voyage on seas
of civil service,
dream shifts into real time,
stories of Eagles' underbelly
begin to unfold.

A long line, millions strong
stretching back to Ben Franklin's vision
of universal service;
connecting every member of a nation
at the lowest cost, the best handling
promoting education and literacy.

The mission to quickly and surely
move the mail was taken up by many
who had been in the armed services.
We novice sailors were told
in no uncertain terms
that this job we did collectively
could not impact adversely
our fellow's workload.

Quickly you were to learn
pull your own weight,
get to work early,
sort the mail quickly,
wait on customers efficiently
(greet 'em and street 'em),
leave your sorting case pulled down
so the next worker didn't clean up your mess.

Until the city's scheme was known by heart
face the case, shut up and sort,
work through sickness, tiredness, boredom.
Don't complain, keep moving, volunteer,
prove yourself a worthy addition
to a very capable, proud workforce.

Carry On

Birth, old age, sickness and death
students of Buddha's teachings
say these are the four marks of existence.
Suffering comes in many forms
yet boil down
to a quartet.

Of the hundreds of workers in blue
they pretty much share a common response
to life's more trying times:
carry on.

Their mission is to carry
happy news and heart-felt condolences,
expected goods and unexpected presents,
keepsakes, trinkets, food, and medicine
sweets just because,
money because it's just.

To every child, woman and man
at every address around the country
and around the globe,
once, sometimes twice a day,
six, sometimes seven days a week,
they carry.

It's what they do.
Sometimes when life is harsh
it's all they can do.
It's what they do best.

For many years they were the most efficient
dependable, trusted, respected
Postal Service in the world,
and they carried it well.

The Numbers Look Good

Saying words that buzz
like flowery phrases
light, flitting, floating,
lacking weight, substance, *Gravitas.*

Line at the bottom of the spreadsheet
demands only to cover one's posterior
while presenting a good face,
shifting blame and onus on to rank defiled.

Ask more with less
precision, without training or support.
Make do, makeshift, make mistakes
highly destructive, highly productive.

Broken backs, gnarled hands, burning wrists
neglected families, blood pressure rising,
drug dependent, diet impaired, sleep deprived,
spiritually adrift, emotionally stunted, alienated.

But the numbers look good
for the current quarter,
and workers just aren't
what they used to be.

A Pound of Flesh

Work, job, occupation, career demand
payment for wages earned:
payback is hell — no fury
like a supervisor's scorn

to make you grovel, beg,
act like a clown, wish you were dead.
When orders come from on high
it's their way or the highway.

It goes against the grain
of sanity, sanctity, good taste,
as it takes something out of you,
ounce by ounce
a pound of flesh.

End of the Line

Before the annex,
prior to the one-queue line
early in my career
there were five long lines.

When one window clerk left for lunch
another would open their station,
take all customers
in the same fair order.

One busy day
I returned to take my co-worker's line.
I opened, everyone moved as one
but one type-A personality barged ahead.

I counted thirty silent seconds
then, in a voice loud enough to be heard
throughout the lobby, said,
"I've waited all my life to be
in a position of power to say,
sir, you cut in, get to the back of the line!"

The man left the lobby
and the lobby erupted
in applause.

Sleeping by the Roadside

Glared and refracted
through hazy windshield, sunshine.
Eyes squint
dangerously close to Big Sleep.

Sirens of Titan calling,
lulling me sweetly
toward cars, sharp like rocks
hurtling swiftly past, in opposite lane.

Lower the windows,
scrunch shoulders, arch the back
shake head, slap face
sing loudly, tap feet.
Nothing staves off the Sandman.

Pulling over
ten minutes into a twenty minute commute home
I drop the seat back, take a nap.
Discretion is the better part of valor.

Sleeping on Benches

Snow blankets the town
but I am safe and warm
deep inside the basement
sorting mail. Suddenly assigned
ten hour shift, end time – 8:30 p.m.

Next, I'm told
to arrive two hours early – 1:30 a.m. —
the next morning.
Only five hours between
punch out and punch in, I'm punchy.

Reeling, I call home
to say I'll be staying in town
at work, deep in its bowels
sleeping corpse-like on a locker room bench
with visions of street addresses,
dancing in my head.

People Are Funny About Overtime

The haves and the have-nots,
a feeling of abundance
a mentality of poverty,
some rejoice at your good fortune
others see it as a threat.

My first few years
many hours sorting mail
along side two senior clerks
who tutored me on surviving
the postal experience.

Lots of good humor and amazing stories
but when the subject of overtime came up
Al and Jerry grew quiet and serious:
"Sully," they said, "if you don't want to make enemies
or get your tires slashed, don't mention
how much overtime you're getting.
People are funny about that."

Bully on by, Levon

Levon was a character and a half,
a mail carrier who reveled in revolutionary war reenactments
taking old, cantankerous and crotchety
to new heights.

Standing too close, never cracking a smile,
and uttering unveiled threats,
was his way of testing you
but I grew less patient for his games.

One tense passing in the work aisle
he came hard at me with his mail satchel,
trying to push me over.
I strengthened the left side of my body,
concentrating chi energy…

Levon's force was redirected,
he spun out of control, landing tortoise-style.
Over my shoulder… I looked back,
glad to no longer
suffer his foolishness.

I've Seen You Before

From some watering hole,
gathering, weekend celebration, memorial,
festival, shindig or hoedown —
can't remember which — I know you.

You're the one who sells stamps
the guy behind the counter,
the dancing postman!

I know you're not at work
so if you don't mind
I've got a postal question for you...

Sorting in the Groove

Sometimes stars align,
biorhythms attune
coffee pumps through veins,
sorting in the groove
addresses, scheme makes
perfect sense — letters
fly into cases
very present tense.
Eyes scan to next,
last piece not settled
in previous slot.
Minimum effort.
Each address ignites
synapses, sending
letters towards a point,
in space before me,
not a route number.
Reach that state of now
flowing one-pointed,
speeding carriers
to appointed rounds.

Self-Study Circumambulation

For too long, window clerks went through
self-study modules in a very hot room,
the Civil Service Room, upstairs, that would lull
men to sleep with its stuffiness.

The secret was to pace around,
circle the room
while reading the text aloud,
jumping as needed
to be tested at the end of these
circular postal reasonings.

To my surprise, there appeared one paragraph
standing out from all the rest —
the mission of the postal clerk
boiled down to its very essence:

You are to give the public
the most efficient, courteous
cost-effective service possible.
Awe struck, I walked downstairs to find my Postmaster.

Confessing, first my ability
to sell a farmer the paint off his own barn,
I inquired: "Do you really want me
not to sell unneeded services or supplies?"

To which he said

"Yes, sell them what they need.
Save them money, time, and headaches,
and they'll keep coming back
for great service."

Well, this changed everything
for me — and my customers!

To Those We Gained

I have never known
a better crew assembled
than the men and women
of the Ithaca post office.

They were up to the Herculean task
of moving ton, after ton, after ton of mail
efficiently, precisely, with good humor.

Floods, hurricanes, cold snaps
dogs, dog days, holidays
weekends, early mornings
late nights, cold and flu seasons
broken bones, broken hearts
broken spirits, they soldiered on.

They accomplished very much
with very little.
Our first Postmaster General,
Benjamin Franklin smiles
on his protégés.

Shape Up
Or
Ship Out

Family

In the heart's core
is a whispered yearning:
provide for those closest
most dear, of deep connection.

It is a strong reason
to put oneself in harm's way,
test physical limits,
emotional balance, spiritual resolve.

Being wed to Esther, just over a year,
before I married the Postal Service,
there grew a strain on our bond
that she would not bear for long.

Only five years later,
her wisdom, compassion, and kindness
informed the decision to separate,
though it fell upon her, the bulk of child rearing.
She always looked out for herself and the children.

Emily, my stepdaughter, was and is
brilliant, confident, and mature
beyond her years.
Sean, my son, a warrior in another life,
was part daredevil, part defender of the innocent.

I lost what I cherished most,
working overtime and days-off
became my substitute
for full-time
fatherhood and partnership.

Recovery Reminders

Thousands of friendly ghosts
haunt the post office
down through the years.

They appear with little or no warning
anonymously bringing
my wandering-ricocheting mind
back to reset and into focus.

Their very presence —
drunk, dry drunk, or sober —
reminds me of who I was,
and what was at stake.

We, this open secret
brother-and-sisterhood suffer
a *dis-ease*, but together we stand
one thousand times stronger
than we once did alone.

It's Not for Me to Judge

The path so long and winding:
chances had been given
a second, a thousandth time.
By all rights I should have died, years ago.

A life preserver was thrown:
I latched on
with the fervor of a drowning man
going down for the third time.

Many years had passed:
I smelled the telltale stench of beer
at 8:30 a.m. when we opened for business
and the first customer needed a money order.

Then there was the exhale of pot smoke:
a courier walked right up
to the counter, without waiting,
oblivious or paranoid
at my recognition.

Another brought the slurring:
the struggle to marshal forces —
logic and clarity — through the fog
of painkillers, and heavy tranquilizers.

Their paths were long and winding:
some will take that thousandth chance
and some will die drunk, but —
it's not for me to judge.

The Ghost of Christmas Past

In water-torture time
most people's favorite reindeer
played continuously in the lobby
to sell the postal holiday video,
images flickered.
Slowly, the endearing tale
wore away my resolve;
I was more than ready
to divulge information beyond
name, rank, and serial number.
To my rescue came
my fellow window clerk
with the *Miracle (on 34th St.)*
and three versions of *A Christmas Carol.*
Alastair Sim and George C. Scott
saved my Christmas goose;
Mister Magoo and Jim Backus
made me ponder
the true meaning of Christmas.
That timeless Dickens tale
brought home the justice of karma,
and fresh hope that all
was not lost, no matter
how far one had strayed.

Christmas Rush

Some gauntlets are harder to run than others,
some seasons longer, more intense
add hours to weekends worked,
mixed generously with sugar and caffeine.

Here's a cocktail, a recipe for failure,
frayed nerves, a dual exasperation.
Shipping late on lines that snake
through the lobby and out the door,

"Hi, may I help you?" shortens to "Next,"
snapping fingers, whistles,
plus cattle prodding tactics
to keep the herd moving through the narrow gate.

And after one hundred too many times
of giving change before payment has appeared,
or calling the next person while the current one
is still preparing to move on,

you snap. People become tormentors.
Survival dictates: "greet 'em and street 'em" —
even friends and acquaintances lose healing powers,
become necessary evils during the season of joy.

Voodoo Child Carol

In moderation, Christmas songs
strike a common chord for many,
harkening back to simpler times,
to an unfettered experience of hope.

In system overload, they strain
the ears with jarring juxtapositions
between what is and what should be
sensations felt during Advent.

In this state of aural bombardment
when jingles scream in singsong rhyme,
a call goes out for electric guitar,
some gnarly, muscular picking,

Feedback as antidote
to sugar-sweet poison
holding sway over airwaves,
this is what I needed:

"...I said, I didn't mean to take up all of your sweet time
I'll give it back to you one of these days
And if I don't meet you no more in this world
Then I'll, I'll meet you in the next one
And don't be late, don't be late... "

- Jimi Hendrix

Jimi Hendrix. Jimi Hendrix The Ultimate Experience.
MCA Records, 1993. CD.

Big Brother is Watching

In each post office of a certain size
there is a secret door
into which only a select few
may enter and ascend, a staircase
that leads to a catwalk
with two-way mirrors on each side
for watching workers
who might be stealing
to observe drug deals
or possible violence brewing.
One day as I was sorting the mail
I smelled a hint of cigarette smoke.
The use of tobacco products
had recently been forbidden
in all federal buildings.
Looking up at the two-way mirror above
I stated: "If you put out the cigarette
or just leave the building,
I'll start working again.
I can wait…" and I stopped sorting.
The smoke odor began to lessen,
so I began to sort again.

Even on a catwalk
one is not above the law.

Stock Audit

Sharpened number-two pencils in a row,
inventory sheets all aligned,
two copies for window supervisor and clerk
calculators and rubber thumb grips, at the ready.

Personal stamp stock — the responsibility
of the individual clerks — in separate drawers,
separate keys fit no one else's lock,
you're on your own: shortages
come out of your pocket.

Overages — another story —
go into the general fund
unless correlation can be made
to another clerk's shortage.

False hopes and false fears
dance their dance
as the sums grow steadily closer
to ominous, final count.

If the total lands beyond tolerance,
another, more painstaking reprise
of the first go around follows.

One's self image is dictated
by entries, columns, and totals.
You were either conscientious, dependable, precise
or an unfaithful servant, reckless with company funds.

Senior Circle Circulars

I've come across
many great sorters
in over a quarter century.

For over two hundred years
the postal exam has tried
to evaluate this unique skill
among millions upon millions of applicants.

The debate still rages:
who was the most accurate,
industrious and enduring,
adaptable and versatile,
and who had the smoothest stroke?

When it came to blinding speed
few could rival or even come close
to the legendary Sally.

Some detractors would point out
her tendency to fill a case (no easy feat)
and move onto the next,
without properly pulling down
the mail from the first,
tainted her records.
Like baseball's steroid scandals
there will always be naysayers.

On one glorious, late winter's day
some twenty two years past
I came into the flat sorting section
feeling particularly frisky, borderline cocky, in fact,

when a full cage of Senior Circle circulars
was wheeled in by a friendly mail handler.

In those days, Senior Circles
were magazine-sized folds, only thinner,
bound for more households
than any other publication
except Pennysavers and political flyers.

For some strange reason, they were my forte.
Maybe it was the rubber thumb grip I wore
or the dancer's rhythm I maintained
on the flat case rubber mat
but I was born to sort them.

Knowing this, I proposed a challenge:
I would sort more USPS plastic tubs
(which, if you have any stashed away
at your home or office,
not being used for mailing purposes,
please return them immediately —
it's a federal offense),
yes, more USPS plastic tubs brim-full of circulars
than Sally could sort, in one hour.

Fearless, calm, and serene
she took the challenge and the bait.
Maybe the stars had aligned just so
or maybe, just maybe she allowed
this better than average sorter
to go toe to toe, *mano a mano* with greatness …
and emerge victorious.

Degraded Mode

Lights on, alarm off
lights on, alarm off again,
unlocking doors, arranging office
for daily public opening.

Never remotely enough time
to prepare for business day dawning
bright, shiny, and new:
less staff, no janitor, scant time
between punch in and first customer.

Not all mornings were created equal.
Computer on, small icon alert:
slow-moving computer.
The dreaded *degraded mode.*

Here a parallel universe
stretched sixty-second transactions
to three or five minutes,
five minutes stretching to ten.

Such rare delays occasioned
a switch of clerks:
one would shut down and reboot
while another stood in their stead.

Customers would walk out, those who
allotted a short in and out amount of time
before work and on to their next appointed round.

Once new clerks had weathered
five to ten of these storms
they became old hat,
but in the meantime my learning curve
was embarrassing and degrading.

I'll Be Late Today, Again

Dark, early morning drives
done in a trance
shaking off sleep
and remnants of a dream
commuting at un-godly times,
there is the desire to give
as little of one's life as possible
to one's job, when so much
has already been taken away.
Here comes the desire to push the envelope,
to stay home until the very last moment,
then to drive too swiftly
on almost deserted roads, taking chances.

And here lies Tim's legend:
no matter how slow, how fast,
which headlights,
various makes or models,
deer whistles and cowbells he used,
his name will live in infamy
as the clerk who was late
forty-two times, because
on the way into work
he hit a deer.

Don't Go Into That Room Alone

Secret police work and dwell
in darkness, weaving intimidation and lies,
living to ruin reputations,
learning to set up, to entrap,
like giant spiders descending from on high
they ensnare workers in a web
of deceit, bullying, and harassment,
waiting and wearing down the will to resist.

Too often they are unleashed on
the weak and the vulnerable.
Time after time, union members warned
against meeting postal inspectors
without representation,
"Don't go into that room alone!"
Yet, like some slow-motion horror movie
they walked into slaughter
and their work world
ceased to exist.

One Number Off, Five-Week Delay

Five simple numbers in a letter can fly
straight to any address in the U.S.,
but a 1 mistaken for an intended 7
can send it 1800 miles off course.

Upon arrival at the wrong post office
the letter is put aside for rerouting.
If the office is large, busy, and understaffed
that letter will be stockpiled.

For the facility, being shorthanded,
JOB ONE is
getting first-class mail out on the street,
each day collecting letters and packages
to go out each night for dispatch.

It's all about looking good.
Numbers concern management.
Other parts of the picture are ignored
so that someone's letter that is misdirected
can sit for five weeks,
with thousands of other letters
until there is a lull
for the few workers remaining
to get around to it.
This is always a great tragedy
that comes as collateral damage:
downsizing to the point of sabotaging the service,
so the post office could be privatized,
and some fat cats could make a killing,
at the people's expense.

Say Nothing, Wait

During dark times
our union president was suspended
for a year and a half.
Through a legal process he had to battle
to be reinstated.

I was called as a character witness.
Our union lawyer warned that I would be attacked.
He counseled calmness: wait for the arbitrator,
do not respond to wild accusations by management.

Sure enough, as my testimony started
a supervisor left the room to get my personnel file.
I was asked if I had admitted
to a drug and alcohol problem on my application.

Furthermore, could not said problem have impaired
my judgment and memory on the days in question?
Well, the manure hit the proverbial fan,
the room exploded with shouting.

I waited quietly, looked at the arbitrator
and asked if he'd like a response.
He said yes, so I serenely recounted
my active addiction until three years prior
to my postal appointment.

I was now fifteen years clean and sober —
which was more than anyone else
could say at the local post office.
The arbitrator chastised management
and reinstated our president.

Beauty
Takes One's Breath

Cloud Bank Waterfall

How many sights and sounds would I have missed
had I not signed on the dotted line,
joined the service, put in twenty-seven years
moving pieces of paper along their way.

One of the sweetest and most surreal
was an early Saturday morning
descending Route 13 South towards Stewart Park.
I was blessed by a morning fog,

flowing down into the lake
in terraced steps like water
crossing huge flat rocks
in mid-air.

Sunrise Tree of Glory

Saturday morning late one fall,
working on stamps-by-mail orders
(pleasant, fast-paced work with
musical accompaniment from my CDs).

Clouds whirled by in snow-laden formations:
heavy greys, hard blacks, but just then
space parted for one focused shaft
of morning sun,
turning leaves aflame:

one remaining remnant
of fall's wardrobe change.

Transcendental Wave of Bliss

With all who approach the counter,
there's me, smiling recognition
of fundamental relationships.

Oceanic waves of all
in righteousness and love
on shores of consciousness.

My forum for musing
on life, love, and letters:
gives rise to repartee
with receptive customers.

"Did you just now feel
a transcendental wave of bliss,
wash over this post office?"

"No? Well it must
have been something I ate
for breakfast."

Early Morning Reunion

Around about 3 a.m.
cars begin to dot the parking lot.
Newly awakened workers put coats in lockers
and pour that medicinal first coffee.

Bright fluorescent banks of light
ablaze above workroom floor
larger than a football field,
while clerks mill around the time clock.

This being a rarity for me
to start so early, after years
of having later window-clerk hours,
I thought I'd break the sleepy silence.

"Have I told you lately
how much I love you guys?
What do you think?
Do we have time for a group hug?"

This was greeted
by a chorus of moans.
Then Pat spoke up: "You've shared a lot
with the people downtown.
We've missed having
you here at the main office
with us."

Dharma Dealings

A scant two blocks
from the post office downtown station
stood a house by Cascadilla Creek —
prayer flags waved in the breeze.

Welcoming front porch,
yard landscaped with care,
intent to radiate
beauty in all seasons.

Two tones colored its sides,
yellow and maroon, the Gylupa lineage
of Tibetan Buddhism.
This was the seat of His Holiness,
the Dali Lama, in North America.

Monks, lamas, translators, students
refugees, bodhisattvas, and Buddhas
all passed through our post office,
and by auspicious coincidence
I was there to serve them.

Snow Lion Press

For centuries, sea mail was the only way
to send letters and goods
around the whole wide world, whether direct
or (more likely) taking a longer route
waiting in each port
for the ship to fill up:
it cost more to move a half-full cargo hold.

The ship might encounter forty-foot waves,
quite a few foot-pounds of pressure
for shifting cargo and precious content.
Books being heavy, they took the brunt
of the impact.

The careful local packers of precious Dharma books
paid special attention to a rare volume
bound for Germany. It received
the roughest voyage imaginable:

battered, bruised, broken, the box arrived,
every book inside crushed to dust
save one, in the center,
the special text, most sacred,
the <u>Snow Lion</u> remained unscathed.

Grassroots Groove

Born of the stuff of stars
energy – mass – total stays the same
connect the dots to all
pixels compose an image
seen nearly as déjà vu.

We have danced before
under other suns and moons
to other tunes primal
songs celestial, raising gaze
towards higher intent and purpose.

No time left for pretense
artifice or sham.
These are the days
of hands joining, of hearts beating
in sync and in love.

There is chopping wood still,
and carrying water
time clock to punch
letters to mail
but my feet are still dancing
and my heart is still singing.

My corporal body is here to serve you
while my astral projection is still
at the Festival, with my tribe —
soon, won't you join me there?

Zydeco Dancing Behind the Counter

Slow tap, quick, quick
slow tap, rock, quick, quick —
rhythm is simply addictive
intoxicating, trance inducing.

Elusive dance step
in sync with partner
moving as one, beat
laid down by drums,
bass and rub board.

Oh to be in a groove, with a room full
of dancers, being one
for a delicious moment in time!

A secret society
spans country and globe.
Acolytes travel hundreds and thousands
of miles to their meccas:
of Lafayette, Monroe,
Breaux Bridge, and Soileau.

It is said that zydeco seeps into your bones
and soul, hour upon hour, listening
doing dishes, dancing in the kitchen
dancing in line, behind the counter, dance.

WRFR (Radio Free Rob)

Music soothes the savage beast.
On the line, in the queue
they have a lean and hungry look.
It's quiet,
too quiet out there.

Two minutes
seem like five
five like ten
and ten like twenty
things to do
people to see
whole lotta livin' to do.

And into the CD slot drops
a sonic vista of another world
low country Delta blues
sweet gospel harmonies
driving Celtic melodies
angst-written, plaintiff protests
songs of love, lost and love renewed.

Timeless tunes, born-again bootlegs,
esoteric and arcane
haunted and haunting
first listens and memory lanes.

The crowd's shoulders drop, stress lessens.
Present a calmer face to the world
toes tapping and thoughts freed up —
towards endless possibilities.

Koko Taylor, Queen of the Blues

At the front counter
you can view a parade of people
amble in, drift out.

Paupers scraping by,
princes from lands afar
mothers wise beyond their years.
Once a Queen, whose coronation
was anointed by soulful singing
of the blues.

She stood back in grace,
in beauty and in humility,
her beaming smile spoke
of the torch she bore
through lineage,
an unbroken chain.

Her sharing of the heart:
the pain of loss
the common thread of missing
a good thing,
felt to the depths
a song lacking filter or pretense.

I called out to her in the lobby
said I'd see the show that night,
thanked her for all she'd done,
and caught a generous smile from a Queen.

World Music, Global Listeners

So much music in the world
too little time to hear it all
there's so much more than what corporate
tells us will sell and must be played.

When a song is good, it's good
in French, Spanish, Swedish, Chinese
Hindi, Swahili, Arabic, Yiddish
Romani, Hungarian, Tibetan, and Sioux.

Ithaca has a certain cosmopolitan flair
and there were smiles of recognition
when favorite songs and genres
were represented in the house.

Expand your horizons beyond the horizon
allow the world to enrich your world
listen with ears and heart
open up to openness,
play, dance, and sing.

Questions and Answers

Moving to Ithaca, New York in 1978
there were many things to learn.
Who ran the town and who ran from town?
How does one fit into the fabric
of community?

Who was in need and who might help?
Where were you welcome and where
should you move through quickly, with game face on?
Without the gift of personal history
it was important to ask, to observe, to listen.

Who sent cards, letters, and packages regularly?
Who gave of their time, their pocketbook, themselves?
Who stood up for their neighbors?
Who had time for strangers?
Who had kindness, patience, and humility?
Who was of service, involved, engaged?
Who knew the secret of life:
to love and be loved
to serve and be served?

Who fell down and got back up?
Who lent a hand and a kind word?
Who was lost for years, then found?
Who thought they had it made
only to end up hollow, empty?

The trouble was, I got to know
many of them, and the respect and love we shared
made their passing
all the more deeply felt.

First Trip to the Post Office

Window clerks have a window
on which to view comings and goings
of thousands of actors in this play
that we commonly call life.

Shining souls orbit
finally drawn towards one another
to merge and bring forth
a separate being altogether.

Often the first trip outside the house
for the infant, is to the post office
where the window clerk gets to say
how very beautiful they are.

Attitude of Gratitude

On most days, on the best days,
there welled up from the depths of my being
an assurance, fundamental and without question,
that I was blessed.

I had gotten what I prayed for
(Lord help me), I was living the dream.
Work tasted like delicious: right livelihood.
There was endless love to give and receive
(if I opened my eyes and heart),
and the job paid more than a living wage.

There was music to keep me company,
there were customers to remind me
one day at a time, easy does it but *just do it
keep it simple* and *don't sweat the small stuff.*

I had health, sobriety, serenity, dance, play,
food to eat, arms to hug, paper and pen,
a radio show to do, friends and family who loved me,
a beautiful part of the world to live in and…

… Finally one more chance to live
my life with the woman I love — Nancy.

Don't Wait One More Day

Snow fell steadily, the crowds thinned down,
we had caught up on sorting, stocking, selling.
On a quiet afternoon, such as this
I would be able to leave early.

Snow had closed the schools, not the roads,
Nancy would be shoveling the driveway,
since today, she was home
like the rest of the school district's staff.

Snow weighed on my mind
as it does on a tin roof,
waiting for warming thoughts
to bring sliding, melting streams —
cares, fears, woes.

Snow stirred up memories and feelings.
Pat, my coworker gave voice
to any misgivings I may have had
concerning a *question that was about to pop.*

Snow piled up outside the window.
Pat talked about relatives we both had lost,
of the brief stay on this earth,
and advised "don't wait one more day."

Snow made driving slower.
I met Nancy in our driveway
with flowers behind my back
and a proposal forming on my lips.

Snow globe scene: me on one knee,
she saying yes, our spirits rising to the skies,
as they have since, each day it snows,
and we shovel together.

A Life
Of Service

Postage Stamps

Mucilage, backing paper portraits
of dead white men
magically becomes ready
to adhere to the upper right corner.

Now, the joy of the mystical,
marvelous, miraculous mission
commences, a handsome
passport across town and globe.

Thousands upon millions upon billions
of epistles, missives and announcements
are carried to the ends of the earth
with an address, a wing, a prayer.

Bringing good news and cheer
to the struggling and worried,
giving hope and support
to the tired and suffering.

A bit of history,
a morsel of culture,
a thing of beauty,
a trace of whimsy,

The stamp heralds,
portends the breadth
and scope of a message —
written, folded and enveloped.

The image of the scene
says as much about the sender
as about the subject
commemorated, depicted and celebrated.

For the price of a postage stamp
one could send a letter
from Puerto Rico to the bottom of the Grand Canyon
to be delivered by mule train.

If the person had moved
it would be forwarded free
to northern Alaska
delivered by dog team.

If they moved again
back to Puerto Rico
another free trip
to finally reach
the addressee.

Not too shabby for forty-nine cents —
an inexpensive way to show
you care.

Maneuvering Other's Energy

Man approached the counter
standing six-foot four, weighing 250 pounds
less than 15% body fat
righteously angry.

He unloaded vehement rage
on this suspecting window clerk
who deftly sidestepped the blow,
throwing the customer off-balance,

"That sounds terrible, you have every reason
to feel angry,
let's see how
we can make this right."

Kiss of Glad Tidings

Wish her well on her travels,
she was with me all those months and years
in the making,
polished and beautiful
into her own
and on her way now.

Late nights walking
the floors and streets,
early morning waking
for caring and tending.

Hard to let her go now
into this world that can be
cruel at times, taking no notice
of small kindnesses.

I entrust her now into your hands.
Send her safely, quickly
on to her new home.
Kiss my creation — be it book, painting, or CD —
for luck.

"It would be my great honor."

Mysterious Mystery Shopper

One would hope for the following qualities
in a window clerk:
warm, inviting, cordial, friendly,
welcoming, personable, accepting,
real, unrehearsed, genuine.
But to score 100% on a mystery shopper's visit,
the following script had to be followed,
less than 100% was not acceptable!

"Hello, is there anything fragile, liquid, perishable, or potentially
hazardous inside this package? – No.
We can send it Express, which is a money back, guaranteed service to
most locations in the United States and includes insurance up to
$100, free of charge. – No
Priority is our cost-effective service, that usually arrives in 2 to 3
business days anywhere in the country, the package could be insured
for damage or loss, up to $5000 or you could add signature
confirmation for security and peace of mind? – No
You say you'd like book rate or the cheapest way possible? Certainly,
book rate is for books and educational materials only. It arrives in 7
to 10 days or more and is usually the least expensive way, would you
like insurance to cover for damage or loss, or signature confirmation
to have a record of who signed for it? – No
Besides this package would you like any philatelic items for the stamp
collectors in your life? – No
Will that be credit or debit? – Credit
I see your card isn't signed. The post office cannot accept unsigned
credit cards. You can either sign it now or provide another form of
payment. – Cash
Here's your change, thanks for choosing the United States Postal
Service. Have a nice day!"

Now's the Time to Express Yourself

There is the dictate to up-sell:
start at the top-of-the-line
and work your way down
to the most affordable.

People tend to zone out —
that deer in the headlights look —
during the first part of an interaction,
so as not to be drawn
into an agreement.

Since I didn't over-push the expedited services,
they knew me to be honest and reasonable.
Once in a great while, a situation
cries out for a guaranteed time of arrival:

Plane tickets for a fast-approaching flight,
first choice for college applications,
grant proposals worth great sums of money —
now's the time to Express yourself.

Save Some Pennies, Waste Twenty Minutes

Bargains, how we do love them!
Deadlines, a rush to wait on line, when
the price of postage rises.
We need to be in that number.

"Time is money and my time is expensive."
"Why aren't there more clerks on today?"
"This is the last day of the old rate,"
irate customers say to me.

"Now let's see, you charge
$200 an hour for your services,
you waited twenty minutes
to beat a two cent increase.
How many rolls of stamps will offset that?"

Deep Regret

There was no excuse for my behavior.
This is how it transpired:
busy morning, only myself at the window,
reinforcements requested and denied.

A young man from another country
sending packages, had many questions
wanted guaranteed assurances
without paying for expedited service.

My patience grew short, as I felt
he was using language as a ploy
for me to prepare his customs forms.
Finally we came to the end of the transaction.

When asked for payment, he realized
his credit card was in his automobile.
He suggested I go on with the next customer
to which I replied, loud enough for everyone to hear,

"No, you're on the computer and I'll lose
all this information. We all have to
wait for you because you weren't prepared.
Go! Can you hear me now! Go!
Get your credit card and come back!"

I proceeded to bark at the next three customers.
They were too scared to complain.
One woman wrote a letter to the postmaster,
she accurately described the scene.

I was then and still am contrite,
resolved not to repeat that behavior.
I do regret that I wasn't able to apologize, in person —
because they deserved better.

One in a Thousand, One Too Many

It is said it takes months to gain a customer
and seconds to lose one.
Once every thousand transactions
there was no filter on my thoughts and words:

The tank was empty
no shade to be found
the joke went too far
past the point of no return

Resentments and hurts that had built up
would finally burst out —
that had little or nothing
to do with the person in front of me.

The 999 customers, to whom I'd been civil
helpful, courteous and kind
meant nothing to the astonished person
before me, to whom I owed an apology.

Penny Wise, Pound Foolish

Our first Postmaster General, Ben Franklin,
was known for many accomplishments.
For one he slept in many beds
and seemed to enjoy his stays.

He also hired many known appointees as postmasters
so that he might have added influence on their work
and many had the last name — Franklin.

He adapted one of the best postal systems in the world
to model our newborn country's service after the French
because we weren't on speaking terms with the English.

Besides,
being an inventor and a brilliant renaissance man
he was known for using wise proverbs.
Rumor has it that he has rolled over in his grave often.

In recent times, many decisions
to cut corners, reduce staff and service
to decrease training and supplies
made "penny wise, pound foolish," as timely as ever.

Two Stamps a Week

Each Tuesday like clockwork
he would enter, smiling a tired smile.
One bill paid, one letter sent,
one short foray into weather prediction, then gone.

Onto the next errand, appointment
and timid smile, trying to stay
in touch with the social niceties
that came with his life before

retirement put a monkey wrench
into the works that ran
like a fine Swiss watch —
his parting gift.

Addressing Addressing to Emailers

Letter writing has become a lost art.
Formats and style are not stressed
or needed in an age of tweets,
IMs, chats, and emails.

So when a high school or college student
was sending their first package
a sense of mystery and quandary
descended upon their face…

With no hint of shaming or blaming
I would say
return address – upper left
where it's going – center bottom
leave room for postage – upper right.
You're doing fine.

You Never Have To Come in Again

Many complain but few have chosen
to take the Golden Nugget of advice.
There was a way around and out
of the frustration they were experiencing.

Short on staff, long on lines,
time wasted behind customers
with huge, complicated transactions
that could take from fifteen minutes each
to the local record — two and one-half hours!

A few suggestions: buy stamps by mail
(delivered to your home for free),
buy a small scale for letters and packages,
use PC postage printed on your computer,
and email for pick up the next day.

We window clerks are a dying breed,
dinosaurs, moving towards extinction.
Learn to mail on your own
and this could be your last wait in line.

Postal Karma Cliché

Why, oh why, do I just get
junk mail, circulars, flyers
credit card offers, sweepstakes chances
addressed to occupant or current resident?

Postal customer, valued contributor
citizen, Mr., Mrs., Ms., hey you!
Sometimes they even have my name
and address correctly spelled.

I don't want them.
How do I stop them?
Please, tell me truly
why don't I get letters anymore?

Well… there is a law of the universe, karma
what goes around comes around,
if you want to receive letters
you must write them.

You Never Win an Argument

Opinions are like a certain body part.
Most people have one.
Those we hold, are not to be cherished:
thoughts deemed true through repetition.

When divergent views collide
discretion becomes valor's better part.
Wisdom and tact counsel public servants
to steer clear of debate.

Can You See Me?

I am a person worthy of respect,
deserving dignity, patience
charity, compassion
your time, energy, and attention.

I am your relation
in this great big, goofy human family.
Treat me like a brother, sister
mother, father, or precious child.

I may not remember
what you taught me six months ago
or understand the instructions,
and have trouble with your logic.

But I don't need a lecture.
Hold your tongue that wants to lash out.
Explain my options for the 10,000th time.
For me it may be my first.

Please be gentle and kind.
Walk me through the process.
I'm here in front of you.
I'm the reason you have a job.

Shall I Supersize That?

Sales are down, down, down
sell up, up, up.

Would you like to open a P.O. Box
for safe, secure, and early access to your mail?
Perhaps some padded envelopes
for your next book sale on eBay?

How about some Disney-themed gift boxes
for the gauntlet of birthdays this spring?
Need a money order for that struggling
college student in your life?
The Year in Stamps might be
the very thing for a budding philatelist.

Try a gift phone card so that cash-strapped
relatives can still keep in touch.
Then there's the — always in season —
packaging tape, because no, it isn't
free in this office.

Cards for all occasions, bubblewrap
for padding fragile items, keychains
with cute logos, colorful boxes for any
and all holidays and events, tubes for posters,
scales for weighing packages
at home, first-day issue sets for
stamps you really enjoyed…

Stamps? You'd just like a book of stamps…
Certainly, we have many books to choose from…
You could collect them all…

Send My Love to Germany

A small percentage of mail is mis-sorted
an occupational hazard, minimized.
A most amazing example passed through my hands
within my first few months as a clerk:

When a letter has a return receipt
there's adhesive on the back.
If not careful, another letter can hitch a ride
and that's how mail from India,
bound for Germany
rested a day in Ithaca, NY.

Not All Are Home Runs

Over two thousand submissions
to mull over and cull through,
anniversaries of significance,
lobbies too strong to ignore.

Postage stamps are a passport
to billions of addresses,
portraits of beauty,
reminders of history.

Raising awareness, bringing smiles
piquing curiosity, but also dismay:
when the French-American Friendship stamp
was unveiled with the French flag colors reversed,

an astute, Francophile postal worker
saw the faux pas and shouted:
"Impossible! This is an affront to
liberty, equality, fraternity!"

Saint Elizabeth

Every saint is a sinner
perfection is an ideal, an inspiration.
Their love of service and self-sacrifice
for the greater good is their hallmark.

To attain sainthood as a window clerk
you need patience which surpasses all understanding,
respectfully listening to complaints,
questions, comments from all sides.

Grace under pressure would be an asset.
Flexible, not just part-time, but full-time.
If you can't take a joke
you don't belong in the post office.

There were many who came close to the ideal,
but the one who came closest was Liz.
First I'd ask *what would Jesus do*
then I'd settle for *what would Liz do.*

She was an easier act to follow.

Christmas Day Delivery

There was a year, late in my career
when I volunteered to work all ten holidays,
thinking someone with a family
could spend more time at home.

It took my mind off my lack
of a son, wife, and stepdaughter.
There was also an element of fun
and a challenge to get the mail sorted.

The tenth holiday was Christmas.
I came in extra early
so I could drive south to my sister's home
for a dinner which couldn't be beat.

I was asked to deliver a few Express pieces
on my way out of town, which was fine with me.
The last stop was a trailer park.
When I arrived, three kids started bouncing off the walls.

Their mom answered the door and signed
for presents from their dad, who couldn't be with them.
She said; "I'm sorry you have to work on Christmas Day
but you just made three kids very, very happy!"

The drive on, to my own Christmas dinner now attained
a lush, warm glow that connected me to childhood —
and to personhood beyond distance
through time — towards an imperfect happiness.

Muted
Musings

Mailman Acknowledgment

Groups of youngsters would tour the post office.
Most often I was their guide,
trying to give them a glimpse
of the magical, mystical movement of mail.

For this reason, when our local author,
J. Robert Lennon, was researching for his book "Mailman,"
I was selected to give him a tour
and answer any questions he might have.

Little was it known that the book
was about a mail carrier (in a city
much, very much, like Ithaca)
who went over the edge…

I had always maintained that the Postal Service
could eat you up and spit you out
if you lacked a strong spiritual foundation,
a wide support system and something more than your job
to bring you identity and worth.

Many workers near retirement found themselves
feeling alienated, cheated, harassed,
worn down, unappreciated, belittled,
hopeless, helpless, angry, vengeful, and alone.

Not a good platform for dovetailing
back into civilian life,
but a great recipe for a character study
and a solidly good book.

Mister Lennon was gracious enough
to acknowledge me,
along with the union stewards
I directed him to interview, in his book.

Fortunately, or not,
the Postmaster General and regional supervisors
didn't read it, so there was no fallout
from my ninety-minute tour of a mailman's mind.

Please, Mister Postman

In a time-sensitive outfit
there will always be much wailing
and gnashing of teeth when the door
bangs shut at the end of business day.

Looks of death, lined faces that missed deadlines,
customers who would come in the next day
to beg for back-dating postmarks —
but this being grounds for dismissal,
rules were not bent.

When the decision was made regionally
to *end extended hours* around Tax Day,
the postmaster had an astute observation:
"They had three months to get their paperwork in."
Please, Mister Postman.

Letter-Writing Campaign

There are relatives and friends
who need to know
they are remembered fondly
appreciated warmly
sought for their wisdom
supported in trying times,
missed and hoped for.

A letter has vast potential
to influence, encourage, inspire.
It takes time, thought, energy
but it's well worth the effort.

Tangible and tactile, extra expressive,
labor of love, work of art
most welcome visitor to one's mailbox —
too few
red letter days.

Paul Robeson is Laughing in Heaven

One of the great voices
of the twentieth century
was honored and commemorated
on a stamp:
and the irony was not lost on many.

A singer with gravitas and conviction,
he also spoke his mind
political views were too radical,
too socialist, too liberal for many.

They wanted him on the blacklist —
keep him quiet and marginalized.
I'm sure I heard him laughing
with gusto, humor, and verve
when he heard
he'd been honored —
and Joe McCarthy had not.

Four Years of Peace

They were at each other's throats
on two sides of a bruising labor war
yet both were proud and fair men —
they found common ground.

The Big Idea was that
if you treat workers fairly and trust that they need
to take personal days when they ask for them —
there would be less sick time,
less labor grievances, happier,
more productive workers.

The Postmaster looked good simply because
Ithaca had the best numbers in Western New York,
(which was top five in the nation),
and the union had less to battle,
more time to breathe.

The Call in the Night

Ring rang, wrung my hands
voice called across the miles
to bring me up short
as all plans faded and changed.

News surrounded by fear
sliced knife sharp through
armor of having covered all the bases
said all the right things.

When the mind is made up
there's no dissuading it:
my son Sean had made his decision
and now he was gone.

My mind scrambled for order, solace,
my heart broke wide open,
my spirit wished him well,
one foot in front of the other.

The voice of the policeman asked
all the right questions.
I gave all the right answers
hanging up the phone, truly alone.

The Day After

Thread lay broken, line cast off
adrift beyond shore, without anchor
rudder was useless
floating with wind and current.

Only voices of friends
distant yet soothing
memories of better days
hazy hopes of times to come.

One foot in front of the last
one task added to the first
going through the motions
staying in motion.

Harder to hit a moving target
with the next wave of grief
anger, loss, confusion, and pain
plow through fields of sorrow.

Had I covered all the bases?
Done all I could?
Been there for him?
Let him know he was loved?

Yes, and yes again.
It was his life and his death,
his pain and his decision —
His mind was made up.

How is Your Son Doing?

My son was a shooting star
flashing across the night sky
welcomed, honored, befriended
in a life that knocked hard.

Those who knew me, knew
fierce worries, concerns
for his happiness, freedom, safety,
at risk, too soon, too strong.

Chips cashed in, just shy of nineteen
thousands of condolences, prayers, and hugs
made living on possible,
carried me when the path was too steep.

Working with the public, you're out there
front and center, questions kept coming
year after year — "How about this weather?
How is your son doing?"

Some questions are harder than others.

Short Staffed

Lines bring out the worst
in all concerned, at times,
patience, thin as paper,
boundaries hazy and blurred,
speech neither filtered nor civil
on a perfect storm day.

The odds were thirty to two,
the pace had held steady
for nearly three hours.
Then one unfortunate woman
said the wrong thing
at the wrong time
to the wrong clerk:

"I demand to know
why the line is so long!"

To which this clerk replied:
"Well, one clerk's grandson
passed away at her home last night
but she really wishes she could be
here to serve you
and another clerk is in the hospital
with a massive heart attack this morning
but I'm sure serving the public
is his second highest priority.
We're so sorry for the inconvenience today."

With that, the customer backed away
shocked, speechless, shaken.

Bully Pulpit

Through dark recesses
of school days and before
to other lives, in other lands
I remember you,

and your brothers, your sisters
mongering fear and dread
in each stomach's pit,
forcing the meek
to doubt their inheritance,
sucking joy, contentment, and security
from the simple every day.

Now you stand before me
reading the well-worn script
of intimidation and threat,
standing a bit too close,
speech drips blood-red with innuendo.

But I have been here before —
I saw you in line.
We are not strangers.
I see through you
to the cowering child within.

This is your day of days,
you can choose to hear the truth
or be fated to live a life without it
when I say:

"You know the interesting thing
about being a bully,
at the end of your life
you'll wonder,

did your son, brother, wife, or mother
ever really love you,
or did they stay
only out of fear."

To which he shook in anger
and left with a gnawing doubt
that hopefully ate away
at a tired, ill advised path.

Three Months Teaching ATM Skills

Pain grew slowly, steadily
until it blossomed into me,
on my knees, crying
searching for some sort of relief.

It was a bulging disk
between the fourth and fifth
cervical vertebrae, and was
mightily inflamed and tender.

In their infinite wisdom
and bottomless cruelty, I was forced
to drive 40 miles up and 40 miles back,
wincing at each bump along the way,

to see a company doctor
who was incredulous that anyone
in my state would be forced
to travel to confirm light-duty status.

So I sat in the lobby for ninety days
teaching customers how to use an ATM stamp machine
that also weighed and metered packages
using a credit card to avoid a wait in line.

While I was out there
condolences and sympathy abounded
for my very apparent pain,
but one customer offered sage advice:

Guy looked me straight in the eyes
and said: "5% of you is in pain,
95% is not, don't give strength to the 5%,
concentrate on the ninety-five."

Thanks to Guy, Jess, Nancy, Janet, Diane, Deena
and many more healers and friends;
my pain lessened and finally abated.
Customers chose not to use the ATM —
to save our jobs... ha!

And in their infinite wisdom
the post office moved the ATM machine
to Buffalo where it might be used more,
and the lines in Ithaca grew longer still.

Here's Your Paycheck

Each tax season, several customers
would pound their tax returns
down on the counter and proclaim loudly:
"Here's your paycheck!"

To which I would reply
in professorial tones,
"Ah, there is a common example of ignorance,
many have made the very same mistaken claim.

The truth is, this small, amazingly inexpensive
stamp in the upper right corner
is what pays my wages,
and your tax payment has nothing to do with it."

To Those We Lost

The end often comes at times inopportune,
quite unexpected, ill prepared,
cut down in one's prime
or well before years turn golden.

As much of a shock as it is
for us, the observers,
imagine the surprise of surprises
for the actual end-gamers.

It's enough to scare you
half to death,
to buy the farm
or punch out, one last time.

To those who passed before us,
know you are sorely missed,
no judgment passed, no hard feelings:
we remember you —
laughing, joyous, shining.

Let the Guilt Begin

One day, above all others
brings out guilt and obligation.
Express mail usage spikes
around the second Sunday in May.

When she has given you the gift of life —
nurturing, encouraging, instructing
loving, caring, even breast-feeding —
money is no object.

Because Tonight I Dance

Born with the heart of a dancer
I lived for those three or four hours
spent in bliss on the floor,
moving in time to a wealth of music.

Work could be hard, tempers tested
hours dragged, lines relentless.
One thought made short lunches
and nonexistent breaks bearable:

no matter what came at me,
even if I had to stay late,
it would all work out —
because tonight I dance!

Today is the Last

Long lines, bustling activity, short-staffed:
always has been, is and will be,
that way in a busy post office
with no let-up or slow times.

As we remember
what was several times meant to be
a solid, immutable reality,
we cling to history's memory.

Yet the question repeats itself
hundreds of times in dumbfounded amazement,
"Wow, I don't think I ever just walked up to the counter.
Where is everyone today?"

The smart aleck, trickster, absurdist
in me would often reply,
"Didn't you hear the news?
This is the apocalypse, everyone's home
saying goodbye."

Will You Come with Us?

To have a meeting of the minds
and hearts during a transaction
was almost always the goal
and joy for me.

Listening to each concern, in turn
followed by compassion, humor, and action
kept interchanges
from escalating beyond the bounds of decorum.

There were lapses in judgment,
ends to patience, extra exasperation —
yet rarely did they go beyond the pale,
until my seven thousandth day.

On the final day of my career,
a valued, fragile customer
came in with a strong suspicion
that would not release its grasp.

She claimed I had been reading her mail,
stealing it again.
She had friends in high places:
M I-6, Interpol, the Royal Family —

She grew loud and angry,
I could not bring her back to reality.
She said, "Let the police come,
I have nothing to fear or hide."

And so they came
and so she went.
I asked for consideration,
no charges, only escort her
from a disrupted office,
to a busy sidewalk —
and our relief.

Crows Serenade Farewell

Front door opened, even earlier
on last work day's dawning.
Ancient song sung by fifty
shining black, winged souls.

Their relations had flown with me,
between seen and unseen worlds
since the first days of memory
and for life upon life before.

Assuring thought warmed January morning:
they were speaking to me in tongues.
I should stop, look, listen
while sky and landscape opened before me.

Tooling down the road,
favorite song on car tape deck
five or six winged brothers
sang back-up, escorting me.

In the fields, opposite Eco-Village,
they were one hundred-fifty strong,
I drove down the hill in awe,
still not prepared for the chorus to come.

In the parking lot behind the post office,
I stood for five minutes, transfixed
as close to two thousand crows were on East Hill,
serenading farewell and welcoming me home again.

Soaking in the moment of ecstasy,
I reveled in my release, to fly once more,
to let my spirit soar, to listen within and without
to hear the call of God, answer and follow.

Ode to Ithaca

An honor to have worked here,
a place so rare and precious,
city once chosen
to be singled out among the rest.
If the Finger Lakes were the imprint
of God's hand on Earth
His index finger would
point to Ithaca.

Bumper stickers state
it's ten square miles
surrounded by reality.
Pundits pontificate
it routinely makes top ten lists.

More groups are present
than full-time residents;
if there's a cause or concern
it has a following, an ear, in Ithaca.

A power place, a vortex
and no rain on Cornell Graduation
for twenty-five plus years —
talk about knowing people in high places!

Caring for humanity,
a thirsting for peace,
hungering for equality,
to learn, to teach,

with an exceptional
patience for questions,
embracing hard work
but celebrating play:

Ithaca where music fills the air,
and there's dancing in the streets.

Made in the USA
Middletown, DE
11 May 2019